Given to:

With Love By:

Granddaughter,
today is a very special day!
It's a fancy time
to remind you that
I love you!
It is Valentine's Day!

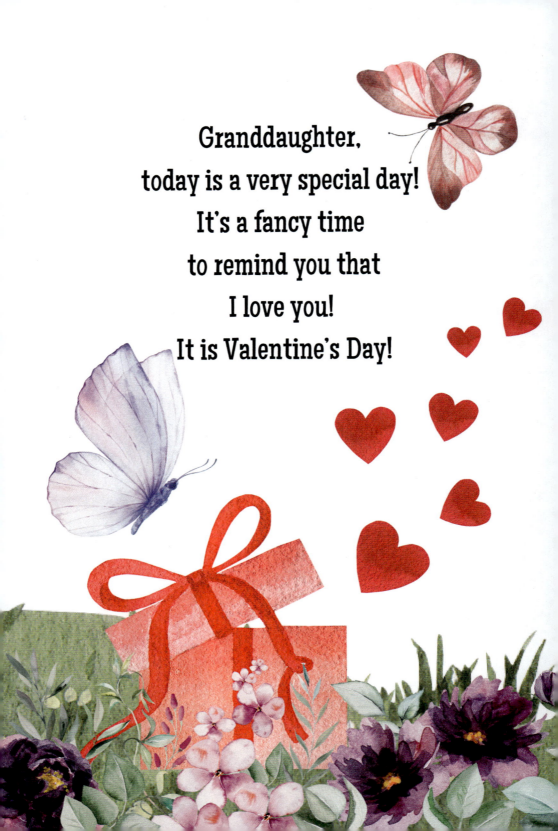

On Valentine's Day,
you may find that some lovely mail
has come your way!

Letters that say how much people care,
can cause a big smile
that is hard not to share.

Valentine Chocolates
are as sweet as can be!
They are as sweet as you
can't you see?

I would love to make a fancy
Valentine's breakfast
to show my love for you dear
Granddaughter!

Valentine's flowers bring joy
for all to see.
They smell as beautiful
as can be!

You are wonderful, my

Granddaughter

dear!
I love you from
your toes to your ears!

Granddaughter,

On this Valentine's Day
I hope you never forget...
That you are so special,
You are so dear,
and I am so blessed
to have you here!

February
14

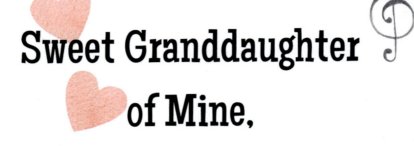

Sweet Granddaughter
of Mine,

**My love for you is like a song
that sings in my heart all year long!**

I hope that this
Valentine's day,
love fills your cup!
I hope that love is overflowing,
so you can fill other's up!

Hugs and notes are good
things to share.
I hope you know that my love
is always there!

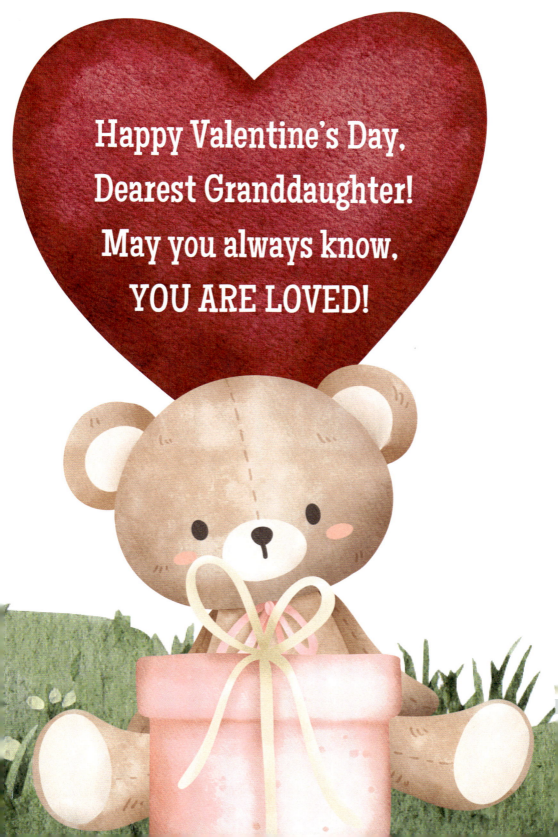

Happy Valentine's Day,
Dearest Granddaughter!
May you always know,
YOU ARE LOVED!

The End

Made in the USA
Monee, IL
06 February 2025

11751956R00017